LURKING BEHIND THE
MASK

VERONICA HARVIN

MILTON & HUGO L.L.C.
4407 Park Ave., Suite 5
Union City, NJ 07087, USA

Website: *www. miltonandhugo.com*
Hotline: *1- 888-778-0033*
Email: *info@miltonandhugo.com*

Ordering Information:
Quantity sales. Special discounts are granted to corporations, associations, and other organizations. For more information on these discounts, please reach out to the publisher using the contact information provided above.

Library of Congress Control Number:	2024907796
ISBN-13: 979-8-89285-076-6	[Paperback Edition]
979-8-89285-075-9	[Digital Edition]

Rev. date: 03/28/2024

Dedicated to my late friend, S Mcgrath.

I extend a special "THANK YOU" to some friends who extended a hand to me when they saw me drowning in a sea of despair.

Sending much love to Debbie A, Frances, Margaret, Carol, Barbara C, Pat B, Joyce, and Tiffany F.

I appreciate and love you all.

Veronica Harvin

BEWARE !

Narcissists are lurking behind alluring masks.

EDUCATE and PROTECT YOURSELF!

I endured 52 years (and still counting) of narcissistic abuse.

I am trapped with no route to escape.

Veronica Harvin

PROLOGUE

I am a 76-year-old woman. I have been married 52 years to the love of my life. My husband is very charming and very likable. He is well respected and much loved by family and friends.

It will be difficult for family and friends to accept the truth I discuss in this book about my experience living with a person who is afflicted with a personality disorder. The journey toward my acceptance that he suffers with NPD (narcissistic personality disorder) was extremely painful and difficult. I am well aware it will not be easy for those who love and care for him to believe me. I speak from my heart. I speak the truth.

The truth is my husband, the man I have loved for 53 years of my 76 years, suffers with NPD. There is no room for doubt. I lived with the painful effects of it for 51 years before the truth was finally revealed to me. The truth emerged after many long hours of research and study. I am not a scientist nor am I a doctor. I am the person who did her homework. I am a wife who endured the ongoing trauma of narcissistic abuse for decades.

I am not inclined to destroy another person's character. I am not inclined to hurt another person by any ways or means. I merely want my story to be told. I want my story to be an enlightenment to others. I want my story to be an education to others.

I want my story to be heard. It is important to me. My story matters because my life matters.

Judge my book in whatever way is your will. Judge me in whatever way is your will. I respect everyone's opinion.

I feel so alone in this world. I live in a world where the ones I love the most on Earth devalued, discarded, and abandoned me. I had a family, but they chose to cast me away as if I were trash. This book confirms my existence. This book says my life matters. This book expresses the essence of me.

Veronica Harvin

INTRODUCTION

I felt compelled to write my story. I hope my story will enlighten someone who is struggling in a relationship with someone who shows signs of narcissistic traits.

I was married 51 years before I realized I was deceived, manipulated, and controlled by a masked bandit who stole the joys of my life. His joys in life were generated by the pain he imposed on me.

I was painfully abused, manipulated, and controlled for decades. My life wasted trying to fill an empty void for the person I absolutely loved with all my being. I did not know he did not possess the emotions needed to sustain a love relationship with me.

There is no love reciprocity in a relationship with a narcissist.

I am writing my story to bring awareness to the destruction of narcissistic abuse. It negatively affects the lives of so many. The effects can ripple down through generations.

NPD (narcissistic personality disorder) is an unfortunate mental health issue. A person with NPD is referred to as a narcissist. A narcissist's life is plagued with feelings of insecurity, emptiness, shame, and self-doubt. He/she develops a false persona and creates a fantasy world for themselves. They believe they are omnipotent. They easily deceive people into believing they are charming, caring, and kind. Their deceptive display of benevolence can lead people to think they are saint-like. However, behind the mask lurks a malevolent being who looks to destroy.

No one chooses to be a narcissist. Speculations are that this disorder develops during early childhood due to childhood traumas. There are possible genetic components linked to the disorder, as well.

Everything in a narcissist's world revolves around himself/herself. They are destructive toward the well-being of others. They have no empathy for the plight of others. They use, manipulate, and deceive others to satisfy their selfish needs and desires. They thrive on causing pain and heartache. Their abusive tactics cause lasting trauma to their victims. Most victims never realize what happened to them. Narcissistic abuse is not a subject people discuss at the dinner table because it is not commonly known.

Some victims are traumatized to the point of suicide; they never get to tell their stories.

I feel so blessed and so fortunate to be alive to tell my story.

There should be education available on NPD. There needs to be an awareness that people with NPD exist in society. People need protection from people with NPD because they destroy lives.

I am not sure if narcissists are aware of their destructive behavior. They just do whatever they want for their own selfish benefit. They feel entitled. It does not matter how their actions or inactions affect others. They have no empathy, sympathy, nor compassion. However, they are skilled at faking these emotions when needed to ascertain what they want from others.

I have written my story of narcissistic abuse because I hope it will help someone. Hopefully, it will reveal some red flags or warning signs that are forthcoming in all narcissistic relationships. There is a pattern that repeats over and over. The narcissist idealizes, devalues, and discards victims repeatedly.

I saw psychiatrists for decades and more recently therapists. I shared experiences of pain and trauma in my relationship with my husband only to be told my husband and I seem to have communication problems. The professionals I saw did not help me.

Professionals need to be trained in NPD. As more victims step forward to tell their stories, perhaps the medical community will be prompted to conduct more studies and to place more emphasis on NPD. Currently there is no cure and no treatment for NPD.

Victims desperately need help. We are struggling to survive the ordeal of multi-faceted narcissistic abuse. Many are dealing with suicidal thoughts and ideations.

Those afflicted with NPD need help, as well. They are deeply troubled and destructive people. However, they are rarely diagnosed and rarely seek help because in their delusional world, they believe they are perfect. They can easily deceive psychiatrists and therapists who are not trained and experienced in the areas of personality disorders.

Please do not let my story be your story!

Observe and listen to the people you meet. There are always red flags when you deal with narcissistic people. Be aware! Educate and protect yourself and the ones you love.

THE BEGINNING

I received my BA degree at New Haven College in spring 1969 after completing my junior and senior years there. It was a cold December evening in 1969. Two friends and I were at New Haven College to hear Adam Clayton Powell speak. As we stood in the hallway waiting, the outer door suddenly opened and in walked this guy who at once captured my attention. He had a sad and forlorn expression. He wore a three-quarter length plaid coat. He was tall, slim, and handsome with an unappealing goatee.

I was a Southern girl straight from South Carolina. My friends were Connecticut city girls. I excitedly ask, "Who is that?" One of my friends recognized him. Her response was, "You do not want to know him; he is married." **(Red flag)**

I should have listened and acknowledged that sound advice: "You do not want to know him." If I had heeded that early warning, my life would have taken a different *course*.

That should have ended my attraction. However, the attraction was too strong. When we were seated, the guy sat directly behind me. This was a time when smoking was allowed in public places. Being a non-smoker, I asked my smoking friend for a cigarette. Then I turned around and asked the guy for a light. He lit so much more than a cigarette for me that night. He lit a light that would glow inside of me for the rest of my life.

I am not sure what came over me. I was strangely enchanted by and attracted to this "married" stranger. It was so out of character for me. I was not the type of woman who would become involved with a married man. That went against my moral standards. Yet, there I was, flirting with a married man.

My friends and I left New Haven College and ended up at a house party. It was there I had my second meeting with Rocky Hudson. He was the strange guy who lit the powerful attractive light inside of me. Rocky told me he was married. He told me he was getting a divorce. He was currently living at home with his parents. Ironically, Rocky lived within walking distance of where I lived.

My behavior that night still baffles me. It was as if a spell had been cast over me. Sometimes, I reflect and think about my life with Rocky Hudson. Could it have been fated by some unknown force in the Universe that cold December night 1969 for my life to be forever linked to Rocky Hudson? Since that night, I have never been able to free myself from the attachment to him.

And so it began, a tumultuous relationship that would affect my life forever. We dated steadily for almost two months. Rocky was so charming, kind, and fun to be with. I was so happy. I fell hopelessly in love with him. I just knew Rocky was the man I wanted to be with forever. **(Red flag)**

I was in a daze. I was in awe over the powerful feelings I had for this man I hardly knew.

I had been charmed by a crafty and masterful narcissist.

We never had sexual intercourse during the first phase of our relationship. Came close several times, but the fear of pregnancy kept me from ever completing the full act.

Then one day, out of the blue, Rocky called and informed me that we would no longer be going out together.

My world was shattered. I thought we had something very special between us. I was bonded and addicted to him. My desire was to be with him as often as I could. I wanted him in my life so badly. I never felt that kind of love for any one before meeting Rocky Hudson. My heart was broken. This was the man I loved so much. Rocky is the only man I have ever loved.

During spring and summer 1970; my body, mind, and soul craved for Rocky. I wanted to see him. I wanted to be with him. I never made any attempt to contact him; I did have self-pride. I never lowered myself to the point where I would chase after a man.

Then came fall of 1970, I had a teaching position and a shared apartment with a friend. It had been over six months since that shattering phone call. I decided to call the number. I made the call and heard the voice I longed to hear. Rocky came back to me immediately. **(Red flag)** He was divorced and still living with his parents. I was elated.

We began having sex on a regular basis. Rocky was my first and is the only man to this very day I have ever had sexual intercourse.

I was completely enamored with Rocky. I loved and adored him so much. I thought he was the knight in shining armor who came to save me. It was many years later before I realized Rocky was the knight in shining armor who came to slay me.

An apartment in the building next to mine was available. Rocky rented the apartment and moved into his own place right next door to me. **(Red flag)**

That's when everything suddenly changed. Rocky never took me out. I would go to his apartment, watch TV, and have sex. That became the extent of our relationship. **(Red flag)**

I was fine with the situation; I just wanted to be with Rocky. I was so happy to merely be in the same room and to breathe the same air as Rocky. My attraction to Rocky was magnetic. I was so in love with this man. I had never felt that way about anyone before Rocky.

Time has proven, I will never feel that way about anyone after Rocky. I have never had any thoughts about another man since Rocky entered my life. The Rocky I loved is etched in my soul forever. He can never be replaced.

Rocky began to distance himself from me **(Red flag)** I soon realized he was entertaining other females at his place. I was young, innocent, and naive. I thought I meant something to him; thought I was special to him. However, it was never like that. I was merely one among many. **(Red flag)**

That was the way it was; that was the way it would always be throughout the 52 years of marriage.

The awareness devastated me. I was so depressed. I felt worthless. I had totally given my love and my body to this man. Desperation led me to swallow a bunch of aspirins. My roommate called Rocky. He came over and said to me, "How do you expect someone to love you when you don't love yourself?" **(Red flag)**

I was traumatized. I packed my belongings and moved to another apartment. I did not try to contact Rocky. However, he found me. Rocky would come to my new apartment to have sex with me and then he would leave. I allowed it to happen many times because I loved Rocky and was happy to devour the tiny crumbs he fed to me. **(Red flag)**

Narcissists use victims.

Then came the day my doctor informed me I was pregnant. When I told Rocky, his response was, "You need to get an abortion; you are not mature enough to have a baby." **(Red flag)**.

The subject of my pregnancy was never discussed again. That was the only conversation we ever had about my pregnancy during the entire nine months. That was a big **Red Flag** that something was not right.

I was miserable and depressed during my entire pregnancy. There was no one to rub my belly; no one to feel the kicks; no one to hold my hand and to comfort me during the pains of labor.

A relationship with a narcissist robs you of the simple joys of life.

I was not seeing the luminous picture of my unusual relationship with Rocky. I was in such denial and so blinded by love. **(Red flag)**

Rocky brought me over to his apartment one time during my pregnancy. While I was there, he was talking with another female on the phone. I threw a glass of wine at him. Rocky quickly jumped up and pushed pregnant me against the wall. **(Red flag)**

I left crying. I was extremely distressed and hurt. I walked several miles back to my apartment. Every step of the way, I was hoping Rocky would drive along, pick me up, and apologize. He never did. **(Red flag)**

Narcissists never apologize.

I wrote Rocky a letter and left it under the door at his apartment. He came home with a female and found my letter. They read the letter together. Afterwards, they called me. Rocky informed me he and the female were getting married. **(Red flag)**

Narcissists abandon victims.

That news rocked my world and nearly drove me to the brink of suicide. I considered driving my car off East Rock.

The abusive tactics of narcissists produce suicidal ideations for some victims.

To survive, I knew I had to go away. I needed to let Rocky go. I needed to focus on myself and the baby I was carrying. It was so evident; Rocky did not care about me and our baby. **(Red flag)**

I attended summer school 1970 at Southern Connecticut State College to complete work on my teacher certification. At the end of summer, my brother helped me drive to North Carolina.

My paternal grandmother welcomed me to stay with her in her three-room house. The first night I slept on the living room floor; a roach crawled into my ear; I went to the emergency room. For the next three months, I slept on the couch.

While I was in North Carolina, my mother contacted Rocky. She was a very out-spoken woman. I am sure her encounter with Rocky was not a gesture borne in kindness. Rocky sent me $100 after my mother spoke to him. There was no message from him, just the $100. It was my only connection to Rocky during my three months stay at my grandmother's house. **(Red flag)**

During the last month of my pregnancy, my grandmother had a stroke and was hospitalized. I was alone and frightened. Her neighbors were so kind to me. They helped and supported me. The night I went into labor, a neighbor called my uncle. He dropped me off at the hospital. I was all alone until my little bundle of joy arrived. I named him Charlie. One of the neighbors paid for a taxi to bring Charlie and me back to my grandmother's house.

Charlie was born November 10, 1971. We returned to New Haven, Connecticut just days after Thanksgiving. We were living at my mother's house. I contacted Rocky; he invited Charlie and me over to his apartment. This proud mama placed her beautiful baby boy into the arms of the person I thought was a loving father. I was wrong. Decades later, I realized those were the arms of a sick, delusional man who systematically poisoned my son's mind against me with his fabricated and delusional lies.

Rocky was a very heavy drinker. He would drink, drink, drink, and then fall asleep. One night he wanted me to come to his apartment. When I arrived, another female was knocking at his door. There was no response. **(Red flag)**

I told her Rocky had probably been drinking and had probably fallen asleep. Very soon after my arrival, the door suddenly opened.

Rocky did not appear surprised to see two females standing outside his door. **(Red flag)**

We both entered. I sat on a single chair. Rocky sat at one end of the couch and the female sat at the other end. The mood was uncomfortable. If the female had been extremely attractive, I would have felt self-conscious and intimidated. However, she was not. I felt emboldened because I had just had his baby. I thought, surely, I was the person he loved.

I was so wrong; I did not know the true Rocky. I was deceiving myself. Rocky did not care about me nor the other female. We were merely names on his supply list of females he could call at any time.

I decided it was best for me to leave; so, I excused myself from the situation. Rocky did not encourage me to stay. **(Red flag)**

I always kept respect for myself. It was not my role in life to be one side of anybody's triangle.

I am convinced Rocky lured us both there at the same time for reasons only he knows. Apparently, the female was someone he had been seeing. She did not know he and I had a newborn. He told me the female removed all her clothes after I left. She wanted to have sex with him. He said he declined because he did not want to lead her on nor to hurt her. He expected me to believe whatever lie he told. **(Red flag)**

Sadly, I always believed him. I had yet to learn what a skillful liar Rocky truly was.

Narcissists have no boundaries.

Another night, Rocky convinced me to stay overnight in his apartment. When I returned to my mother's the next day, she berated me and said I was going to have another baby. I was crushed and ashamed.

I was a Southern girl. Born and raised in the Bible Belt South. We were the "good girls"; Southern girls did not have illegitimate babies. That was a disgrace to the family. I felt a lot of shame and embarrassment during my pregnancy. Being pregnant and single in 1971 was disgraceful; a secret people wanted to keep behind closed doors.

These events happened during the early weeks of December 1971. Charlie was one month old.

I knew it was time for me to move forward. I was so blessed to have a principal who knew I was pregnant and single. My principal, Mr.C, helped secure my teaching position. He replaced me with a substitute teacher until I could return to work in February 1972. I felt blessed. I was grateful for his gesture of kindness and concern for me when I so desperately needed help.

It was Late in December 1971, time to focus on my future. I called Rocky and told him I would not be coming over anymore. I was ready to begin life with Charlie and me. I was again prepared to let Rocky go and to move forward without him. It was so much easier to let go now that I had Charlie in my life.

I did not expect to hear from Rocky again. A few days later, Rocky came to see me. I got into his car and Rocky said, "We're going to get blood tests so we can get married." Just like that! I was naively elated. A dream comes true! A prayer answered! I gleefully agreed. No questions asked; no explanation needed. Where was my mind; what was I thinking? Huge **RED FLAG!**

My thoughts were that Rocky genuinely loved me; he wanted to marry me. You only marry someone you genuinely love. My interpretation of love was so skewed. I did not know what true love looked or felt like.

Rocky took me on a shopping spree; bought new leather boots, a new coat, and a new dress for the marriage ceremony. My happiness was beyond any words I can use to describe. **(Red flag)**

Narcissists manipulate victims.

Rocky's parents lived just walking distance from where each of us lived. I met his parents for the first time after we were married. **(Red flag)**

It never entered my mind that it was odd Rocky did not introduce me to his parents prior to our marriage. My overwhelming desire to be with Rocky superseded any other thoughts I had about our strange relationship.

Narcissists are secretive.

I see now there was never anything in the range of normalcy about the relationship between Rocky and me. None of the strangeness registered in my mind at that time.

Today, there stands a luminous projection of so many red flags I missed along the way in my relationship with Rocky Hudson.

December 27, 1971, was once considered the happiest day of my life. It was the day I became Mrs. Rocky Hudson. It felt as if I won the lottery. Rocky was the jackpot and I won him. I felt like the luckiest woman in the world. I felt so fortunate.

I reflect and see how warped my thinking was when it related to Rocky Hudson.

It was decades before I realized that was the day I entered a world of fantasy created by a master manipulator. Rocky never loved me. In time, he would destroy the essence of me. I was unable to see all the forthcoming warnings to the decades of abuse that were looming in the future for Charlie and for me.

DONNA DRIVE

Rocky moved us into a new apartment on Donna Drive, New Haven, Connecticut. No chance for females to show up knocking at his door. My happiness was beyond anything I could have imagined. I loved Rocky so much.

I ignored the fact Rocky routinely stayed out late every night on the weekends. It became what was normal; I accepted and expected it to happen. Rocky claimed falling asleep drunk at relatives' homes was the reason he was always returning home late hours. **(Red flag)**

I innocently believed Rocky. I was his wife; I thought he loved me. I did not know what Rocky was doing was not what a loving husband does.

Narcissists are entertained by their deceitfulness.

I innocently believed Rocky's lies for the next 12 years we lived in Connecticut. I had no clue Rocky was lying, cheating, and deceiving me all those years. He had me well programmed to believe all his lies. I thought he was a loyal husband. I thought we had a normal relationship. I was so deceived. I was so naive. I was so gullible.

I was the puppet; Rocky was the skilled puppeteer.

I desperately wanted to have another child. Rocky convinced me to get an IUD when we first got married. **(Red flag)**

The IUD damaged my body. I was never able to have more children.

I found out Rocky was having unprotected sex with multiple women all during the marriage. This awareness spawned wrenching pain in my heart, in my soul, in my mind, and in my spirit.

Rocky's influence and control cost me the ability to ever become a mother again. What an astronomical price to pay! I will never recover from the devastating cost.

Narcissists control victims.

Rocky had a son, William, with his first wife. William spent a lot of time with Rocky's parents. However, I never knew nor saw Rocky spend any time with William before we were married. **(Red flag)**

After we were married, William often came and stayed with us on weekends. One weekend after returning William to his mother, Rocky came back in tears. He said William's mother said she thought it was best for William to live with us. I told Rocky to go back to get William. William's mother gave Rocky full custody.

Our little family increased to four. I was happy to become William's second mother.

There was a strange event that occurred in my life two years before that cold night in December 1969 when I first met Rocky Hudson.

I did not realize until after Rocky and I were married in 1971 that our paths had crossed back in 1967. I went on a one-time date with the guy in 1967. Later, I learned the guy was a distant cousin to Rocky. This date included multiple couples. They all knew each other. I was the stranger to the group. We stopped at a house to meet up with another couple. The wife was waiting for her military husband to arrive home from New Jersey for the weekend. The couple had a beautiful infant baby boy.

The soldier arrived; we all went together to see the movie, "Me and Mrs. Jones," and out to eat afterwards.

I did not have any interaction with the soldier and his wife. I did not remember their names. I just remember thinking how lucky she was to have a husband and a baby. I never saw them again.

Well, it was quite a shock when I realized in 1971 "that soldier" was Rocky Hudson. The infant was his son, William.

When I met Rocky in 1969. I did not recognize him as the soldier I saw back in 1967.

My mind cannot process how and why our lives were intertwined in such a strange way.

At the beginning of the marriage, Rocky was adamant that we pool all our money together in one pot. **(Red flag)**

I willingly put my paycheck in the pot for my entire thirty-year teaching career. I also brought into the marriage a $1000 investment I made during my first-year teaching. One thousand dollars was a lot of money in 1971.

Rocky and I did not have separate bank accounts. I thought it was perfect; we shared it all. I thought we were an exceptional couple. Rocky had total control of all finances; he paid all bills. **(Red flag)**

Narcissists treasure control of money.

As the years progressed, I made many financial sacrifices for the family. I bought a sewing machine and made some of my clothes. In later years, I bought clothes and shoes at thrift shops.

Rocky was spending, buying, and doing whatever he wished with the finances. I foolishly never questioned anything he did; I trusted him completely. **(Red flag)**

Narcissists love to splurge on themselves.

I learned a valuable lesson too late. You should always keep an independent bank account for your personal protection and security.

Always have a nest egg to protect yourself from the narcissist thief.

When I returned to work in February 1972, Rocky worked nights. He gladly opted to care for Charlie during the day. I often wonder if Rocky neglected Charlie when he was tired and annoyed by the demands of an infant. I shudder to think about the possible abuse Charlie might have experienced during his first months of life.

Some days Rocky brought Charlie to my job during my lunch hour. It was during this time I received phone calls when I got home from work. A female called to tell me Rocky had Charlie meeting with his girlfriend at a park near where I worked. **(Red flag)**

I did not believe her; that just could not be true. My Rocky would never do that. I confronted Rocky; he denied it; I believed him. I had yet to learn that my Rocky was a master of deception. **(Red flag)**

Narcissists are skillful liars.

HOOP POLE ROAD

About a year after we were married, we were able to buy our first home on Hoop Pole Road, Guilford, CT.

Hoop Pole Road was too far for folks to visit. A phone call would cost you. I was isolated in a predominantly white community with two small children. **(Red flag)**

Rocky was working days. He was home most weeknights; but come weekends, he was gone, not seen nor heard. He stayed out late every night during the weekends. I simply accepted it as his routine. I guess I thought that is what men commonly did. I did not know it was not the norm for a devoted father and husband. I had no experience with life in a traditional American family unit. **(Red flag)**

I was stressed and anxious all the time. I was struggling to work full-time; to care for two small children and to maintain a home. There were no friends nor family nearby for support. **(Red flag)**

Rocky was enjoying his frequent jaunts into the city while his family remained isolated in an unfriendly community. He was enjoying doing whatever he was doing for those long hours away from home. The children and I were left to fend for ourselves in isolation far from family and friends. **(Red flag)**

Narcissists isolate victims.

One night, while living at Hoop Pole Road, I was fed up with Rocky's late-night adventures. I locked all the doors from the inside so Rocky could not gain entrance when he returned home. When Rocky realized all the doors were locked from the inside, he simply went around to the back of the house and busted out one of the windows to gain entrance into the house.

Narcissists rage when denied.

AIMES DRIVE

More than a year later, Rocky got a promotion to White Plains, NY. We considered moving to New York, but settled in West Haven, Connecticut. It was a blessing we remained in Connecticut because we would need family support during our stay on Aimes Drive.

While living on Aimes Drive, William was diagnosed with leukemia. Having a child with a possible terminal illness did not deter Rocky's behavior. He continued to be absent from home; staying away for long hours. I never knew where he was. **(Red flag)**

We argued often and a lot. Rocky did not provide the support his family needed during that pivotal time in our lives. He continued to pursue his wants and desires more than anything else. **(Red flag)**

Narcissists are self-centered.

I realized William's condition was profoundly serious. I began to have bouts of depression and anxiety. I was nervous and fearful all the time. I was a full-time employee and a full-time mom to two precious little boys. One of them had a life-threatening illness. Life was exceedingly difficult for all of us.

It was painful to watch William as he struggled with the effects of treatments for his illness. He was a very brave and a very loving little trooper. He never complained. It was heartbreaking. Life was a tremendous strain for the family and for everyone who knew and loved William. We lived with the painful awareness every day that William's prognosis was not good.

William died nine months after being diagnosed. He was nine years old; Charlie was four years old. The loss of William affected and devastated many people.

There were too many sad memories at Aimes Drive. The pain of William's absence was too overwhelming. We decided to move.

UPPER STATE STREET

We settled on Upper State Street, North Haven, Connecticut. Shortly after moving in, I found out we lived down the road from one of Rocky's former high school girlfriends.

She was married with kids. However, it was well known that their oldest child was Rocky's biological son. My understanding is that Rocky discarded her when she was pregnant. Another guy stepped up and married her. **(Red flag)**

Narcissists are not responsible.

I believe Rocky purposely moved us to Upper State Street. It fueled his ego to have his wife and son and ex-girlfriend and son on the same street. **(Red flag)**

Narcissists are egocentric.

We were struggling to adjust to life without William. It was extremely difficult. During this time, Rocky became more and more emboldened with drinking and staying out late nights. He was very cold, distant, and unaffectionate. **(Red flag)**

We were having serious marital problems. I could not give up on the relationship. I loved Rocky so much. So, I tolerated his behavior because I could not face the possibility of living my life without Rocky. He was my addiction. **(Red flag)**

We were living on Upper State Street when Rocky began talking about a female at his job. He was so concerned about her because he did not think she was being treated fairly. I never met her, but I am sure he was having an affair with her. That is the reason he was telling me about her. **(Red flag)**

Narcissists speak revelations.

I am convinced Rocky was seeing other women, as well. There were signs and scents on his clothing during our stay on Upper State Street. **(Red flag)**

I was in denial. I did not want to face the reality that Rocky was cheating.

Narcissists are serial cheaters.

I remember one time we were all packed and ready to go on vacation to New Jersey. The night before we were to leave, Rocky did not return home. That morning, I removed my wedding band; put it on the kitchen table; took Charlie and drove to New Jersey. When Rocky returned home, he found the ring. He removed his wedding band and threw both rings into the woods behind our house. **(Red flag)**

Narcissists are vengeful.

We continued to argue a lot. Once, during an argument, Rocky unexpectedly knocked me down on the concrete floor in the garage. My head hit hard on the concrete floor. **(Red flag)**

Narcissists are impulsive.

I took Charlie and stayed in a hotel for a couple of days.

I was stressed, confused and depressed. I had suicidal thoughts; I had thoughts of killing Charlie and then killing myself. Living in those circumstances with Rocky was fogging my perceptions of reality. I could hardly function. I was in a dire mental state. **(Red flag)**

I began having excruciating and debilitating cramps accompanied with episodes of vomiting and defecating during menstrual periods. I was so sick I had to crawl to the bathroom. If I got my period when I was at work, I had to leave at once or someone had to drive me home.

Narcissists effect mental and physical health issues for victims.

Rocky began priming Charlie at a very young age. When Charlie was five years old, he wrote a note to his father saying, "Dear Dad, I have run away". "Don't look for me". PS "It is all mommy's fault ". **(Red flag)**

Rocky and Charlie appeared to have a very warm and loving father-son relationship on Upper State Street. Rocky often took Charlie to New Haven to visit the relatives who were his drinking partners. Charlie told me tales about those visits. He told me his father and some lady spent a long time alone together in the basement at the relative's home. He told me his father told his relatives the only reason he married me was because of him (Charlie). Heartbreaking tales for a young mother to hear from her young son. **(Red flag)**

Whenever I was in the presence of Rocky's family or friends, my gut instinct felt that something was different and unusual. There was often an eerie feeling of awkwardness. I believe Rocky told friends and family members weird tales about me, delusional stuff he made up in his mind to make himself look like the good person. I think he deceived people to believe there was something lacking in me. **(Red flag)**

Narcissists smear victims.

CROWN ROAD

In 1980, Rocky got transferred to New Jersey. Crown Road, Somerset, New Jersey was a new beginning for us. There were no friends or relatives for Rocky to visit and to stay out late at night. We did manage to share some happy times at Crown Road.

The many arguments continued; life continued to be stressful. One night during an argument, Rocky called me a bitch. I was so upset I started swinging my arms and hands hitting him. Somehow, our hands and fingers entangled as we scuffled. I left the house; when I returned, Charlie told me Rocky was in the hospital. He rode with his father to the hospital and then drove himself back home. He was 14 years old.

I rushed to the hospital. Apparently during our scuffle, Rocky's finger was broken. I was distraught, remorseful, and ashamed. I felt so guilty because I contributed to his injury. It was my fault. I was overcome by my emotions and reacted violently to being called a bitch. **(Red flag)**

Narcissists demean victims.

When Rocky talks about the incident, he says I threw a chair at him. **(Red flag)** I did not have the strength to pick up and to throw any chair that was in the house. That did not happen. However, I understand that in Rocky's delusional mind, he truly believes his version of the incident. **(Red Flag)**

Narcissists are delusional.

Negative encounters with Rocky always evoked a fight /flight mode in me. **(Red flag)** Most times I chose to flee. My choice put me in dangerous situations many times.

Rocky and I attended a party with family and friends one night. I was jealous because Rocky was dancing with other women. After we had a negative verbal exchange, I left walking home down a lonely dark road with no sidewalks.

Luckily, my aunt and uncle pursued me and brought me safely home. Rocky showed no concern for my welfare. He returned home much later as if nothing had happened. **(Red flag)**

Another incident occurred when Rocky, a friend, and I went to a large movie theatre complex late one evening in Milford, Connecticut. Rocky and I had a spat about something. I took flight walking away from a desolate movie complex that was miles from where we lived in West Haven, Connecticut. Rocky's friend found me and rescued me from potential danger. Rocky was content to leave me in that secluded isolated area miles from home. I shudder to think what could have happened to me. Rocky showed no concern or care for my plight. **(Red flag)**

There were many times in Connecticut and New Jersey when Rocky and I were in the car and an argument erupted. I don't recall the reasons we argued; nor why so often. I always felt it was my fault. **(Red flag)**

I would tell Rocky to let me out of the car. He let me exit the car, drove away, and never returned. It could be day or night. I was left on the street to walk home or to find a pay phone to call a friend to come for me. **(Red flag)**

Narcissists have no empathy for victims.

Charlie was becoming a teenager at Crown Road. I think I became overly protective after William died. I was a helicopter type mom, always hovering and protecting. I was always on high alert where Charlie was concerned. Charlie and I had many issues to deal with while living on Crown Road.

Charlie started working at age 14. He chose to begin working at that young age. One day when I took him to work, we had a disagreement about something. Charlie pulled me into a strong grab hold. **(Red flag)** I had no power to release myself from his hold. This is a mother's shameful confession: "I spat at Charlie". It was the only defense I thought I had. I am ashamed to admit I did something so degrading and so despicable. The truth needs to be told.

Throughout his teenage years, Charlie purposely engaged in many tricks and pranks that enhanced my stress and my anxiety. **(Red flag)**

On one occasion, Charlie and I were at a large mall in New Jersey when we became separated. I was in a high state of panic as I frantically searched for him. The mall had two floors. I finally saw Charlie as he descended on the escalator with a big grin on his face. I rushed toward him flailing my arms and screaming at him. He had been watching me all the time as I frantically looked for him. Charlie often expressed amusement as I struggled with confusion, stress and distress. **(Red flag)**

Rocky and Charlie appeared to derive great pleasure seeing me confused and stressed. They laughed at my mistakes and laughed when I could not comprehend something. **(Red flag)** There were times when I felt dumb and stupid in their presence. **(Red flag)**

Rocky was controlling and manipulating us all the time. Charlie and I faithfully followed his directives. **(Red flag)** I did not realize how much of an impact our family dynamics had on Charlie over the years.

One day, returning home from work, I observed Charlie acting very strangely. He admitted to taking some pills in a suicide attempt. He got a bad report from school. He was afraid of what his father was going to do or to say. **(Red flag)**. I rushed Charlie to the hospital where they assisted him to regurgitate the pills from his body.

When I was 40, I missed my period. A few weeks later, I experienced excruciating pain at work. I went into shock and was rushed to the hospital. I had a life-threatening ectopic pregnancy. Rocky rushed to my side. He played the role of a kind, loving, and caring husband. It appeared he really loved and cared about me. It was an award winning performance. Rocky soon reverted right back to his cold and indifferent persona showing no concern for my sad state over the loss of the baby. **(Red flag)**

Narcissists have no compassion for victims.

CHESTERFIELD WAY

In 1989, Charlie finished high school and left to attend college. Rocky got transferred to Atlanta, Georgia. I was excited to move to Atlanta. My childhood friend lived in New York. She decided to move her family to Atlanta at the same time.

By summer 1990, both families were settled in Georgia. Chesterfield Way, Conyers, Georgia is about 25 miles east of Atlanta. My friends, Alice and Jacob, were enjoying life in Lithonia, Georgia just a few miles from us.

Alice and Jacob were New Yorkers; they enjoyed partying and having fun times. It was not my lifestyle, but it certainly was Rocky's. They were the perfect new friends for Rocky. Rocky soon began his routine of drinking and staying out late into the night hours. **(Red flag)** He deceived me into believing he was hanging out with Alice and Jacob when most times he wasn't.

I became frantic one night when Rocky did not return home from Alice and Jacob's. I contacted the Rockdale Sheriff's Department because I feared Rocky, in a drunken state, had an accident on the back road route he drove. The deputy drove along with me; flashing a bright light along the route; searching for any signs of Rocky's car to no avail. I returned home weary and stressed to find Rocky sprawled across the bed. He had been at an Atlanta strip club. **(Red flag)**

Narcissists are accomplished liars

The devastating truth was revealed when I received a call from my primary doctor informing me I had chlamydia. **(Red Flag)** I honestly did not know what chlamydia was; I had never heard the term. I wanted them to provide another reason as to how I contracted the disease; I did not want to believe the true cause.

The shock of having an STD was paralyzing. Rocky was cheating, having unprotected sex and putting my life at risk. The devastation was a massive blow to my self-esteem and to my feelings of self-worth. It should have been the breaking point in our relationship. However, my trauma bond to Rocky at this point was so strong. I could not envision life without him. **(Red flag)**

Narcissists are serial adulterers.

In our personal relationship, Rocky was cold and distracted. He displayed little to no affection for me. **(Red flag)** I began having panic attacks accompanied with horrific dizzy spells. I had feelings of blood flowing from my brain down to my back. It was a horrifying experience. I really believed my death was imminent. I was rushed to the hospital several times. Each time, the result of tests did not reveal any physical causes for what was happening to me. **(Red flag)**

I was referred to a psychiatrist. I began a 30-year span taking anxiety and depression medication. I kept anxiety pills with me all the time. I took them whenever I was anxious or stressed at work or at social functions.

There were often times I took anxiety pills when travelling in the car with Rocky for miles. I felt stressed and anxious. There were feelings of loneliness with Rocky sitting right next to me. There was no interaction and no conversation between us as we traveled hour after hour. It was always so painful. I did not understand. I did not know it was a form of abuse, **the silent treatment. (Red flag)**

Narcissists do not connect with victims.

The doctors never told me the anxiety pills were addictive. I learned about lorazepam addiction after decades of dependence. I did not crave them, but I relied on them as I struggled with anxiety and panic attacks.

I slowly weaned myself off them. The withdrawal was a very scary and a very unpleasant experience.

I truly believed I was mentally ill. **(Red flag)** Being labeled mentally ill gave justification to what I had experienced for so many years. I did not know I was living in a toxic relationship that was slowly destroying me. I had no clue as to what was really happening to me. The emotional, mental and psychological abuse was decades long.

In 2008, Rocky was diagnosed with early stages of prostate cancer. He got treated and was cured. However, the treatment caused him to have erectile dysfunction.

Rocky and I never had an active and exciting sex life like I saw in movies. It was never passionate nor loving. **(Red flag)** I was grateful for whatever intimacy I was privileged to receive from him. **(Red flag)** I did not know any better; I had no sexual experience prior to meeting Rocky Hudson.

I settled for what I got and did not complain. I had no sexual experience to compare. I have never to this day touched or been touched by another man's penis. Rocky is the only man I have ever been with sexually.

Narcissists do not like intimacy.

Rocky never touched me in any sexual way for the next 14 years. **(Red flag)** Rocky had Viagra, but he never took the pills when he was with me. **(Red flag)** Those were some of the most painful years of my life. I think Rocky was having secret affairs during those painful years.

Narcissists have secret lives.

Living at Chesterfield Way, Charlie and Rocky had one major conflict that was quite disturbing. Charlie was home from college. He had his driver's license and was allowed to drive our cars. Charlie did something that caused Rocky to take away his driving privileges. On one particular day, Rocky told Charlie to wash the cars. Charlie's response was, "If

I can't drive it, I am not washing it". Charlie's response caused a rage in Rocky. Rocky went outside and returned inside the house with a pitchfork. **(Red flag)** My heart was pounding. Luckily, Rocky calmed himself and backed away. The sight of the pitchfork and Rocky was profoundly disturbing. I did not think so at that time; however, today my thinking is, **"Was it symbolic to something devious and evil about Rocky"?**

Narcissists are threatening.

CHINABERRY CIRCLE

We bought a house at Chinaberry Circle, Hilton Head, South Carolina. It became my house of unrelenting heartache and pain.

During my research on NPD, 1 learned that a relationship with a narcissist always inevitably comes to an end. The narcissist idealizes the victim; puts the victim on a pedestal. The day comes when the victim falls from the ideal pedestal that was formed by a delusional perception in the narcissist's mind. The victim fails to hold up to the high standards set by the narcissist. Then begins the devaluation cycle. The victim is subjected to multiple forms of narcissistic abuse. The victim is plagued with feelings of depression, confusion, distress, anguish, and pain. The victim is discarded and abandoned . There is no closure for the victim. The heartless narcissist moves on effortlessly to the next prey who has already been primed.

This is a pattern that repeats again and again with every victim of narcissistic abuse. That is the painful cycle 1 experienced repeatedly with Rocky over the years.

When we lived on Chinaberry Circle, Rocky imposed his final discard of me. I meant nothing to him. My only value to him was entrenched in our finances.

That painful knowledge rips through my body as if it were a sharp blade every single day of my life.

In the beginning, life on Hilton Head Island was exciting and fun. I made connections that brought a lot of loving and kind friends into our circle.

I introduced Rocky to a Qigong group. They got him set up to be a leader. Everyone loved Rocky. He was charming, charismatic, kind, and helpful. He happily went to any female's home to help with any chore if he were asked. **(Red flag)** I thought nothing of it and supported his endeavors to help others. I sincerely thought Rocky was always loyal to me on Hilton Head Island.

Narcissists are charming.

There was one female he talked about a lot. He went to her house on several occasions to help her. Those were the times I knew about; I suspect there were other times I did not know about. I always had a strange gut feeling about her. She never made eye contact with me. She was never friendly toward me. However, she was friendly with Rocky. **(Red flag)**

I recall one day at Qigong; Rocky was teaching me to use a video camera. He kept the camera focused on this same female. **(Red flag)** I continued to video as he stepped back in line with the Qigong group practice. The female moved over next to Rocky. They did Qigong movements in sync with each other. I captured the scene on video. **(Red flag)** Thinking back to that day, I feel so used, so hurt, and so humiliated. It was right there before my eyes, but I was too blind to see.

Narcissists feel entitlement.

I was selling an expensive, rarely used exercise bike Rocky bought. He said this same female was interested in buying it. He wanted to take it to her house for her to use to see if she liked it. **(Red flag)** I blatantly said, "No, that is not happening"!

Weeks later, Rocky invited her to our home to show her how to use the bike. I opened the door when she rang the bell. She did not make eye contact with me. **(Red flag)**. My gut feeling told me something dubious was occurring. **(Red flag)** Rocky and the female spent time in our sunroom as he showed her how to use the bike. Sometime later, Rocky walked her out to her car where they chatted for a while. **(Red flag)** That was a painful reflection of his blatant disrespect for me.

Narcissists are disrespectful.

I did not stay to observe them. I was so distressed and depressed; I remained in the bedroom. I felt as if I needed to allow them their privacy. **(Red flag)** Another woman was in my house being entertained by my husband and I felt like the outsider. My mind was so twisted.

It is so insane to think about that as I write now. That is how messed up your mind can become when you deal with a narcissist. Your thinking can become very irrational. Narcissists have cunning abilities to confuse you and to cloud your thinking. It drives you to feelings of insanity.

Narcissists are gifted with skills of manipulation and gaslighting.

I was so blind; I have no idea how long they shamelessly carried on right in front of me. It breaks my heart into pieces to realize Rocky played me like a fiddle while enjoying the music with another female.

Rocky was jovial, happy, and friendly during Qigong sessions. When he and I left, he was sullen and detached from me in the car. **(Red flag)**

Narcissists are cunning.

His behavior toward me became unbearable; I stopped attending the Qigong sessions. He seemed delighted that I no longer attended. (Red flag) He was free to engage and to charm the female members.

Journal Writing I Did Years Before I Knew About NPD (Narcissistic Personality Disorder)

May 29th, 2011

There are those who theorize that writing is therapeutic. With that thought in mind, I embark on a journey powered by the pen.

Today is Sunday, May 29th, 2011. I am here on Hilton Head Island alone. Rocky left this morning, returning home to Georgia. He feels some anger towards me. He threatened to leave yesterday, but I literally begged him to stay and to leave tomorrow as planned.

He reluctantly stayed, which relieved my mind because I did not want him to leave after we just had a disagreement.

His anger was triggered when I complained about the ways he spends money on things not needed. We were going to attend a play at Shelter Cove Park. He bought two new chairs for us to use. I knew there were chairs in the back of the Toyota, so I was really upset that he bought new chairs.

I told him I was happy he was leaving for Georgia tomorrow because we need time apart. I also suggested that he live in Georgia and I stay here on Hilton Head Island. My words fueled his anger to the extent that he decided to leave for Georgia immediately.

People say money is a factor in failed marriages. However, that would not be a cause for Rocky and me. For years we have viewed whatever money we have as ours or so I thought. Marriage united us as one to share equally.

Now is a time in our lives when I feel we must spend less and be more fugal. Our retirement funds are nearly depleted. I was gleeful when we were able to retire early. I thought we were all set for life. Never once did I think that there would come a time when the money well would run dry. I always trusted Rocky's financial decisions; blindly thinking he would always have a plan for financial security.

The blinders have been removed. We are in trouble. I am worried sick about the prospect of being broke and feel heartbroken because we won't have anything left for Charlie and his boys.

I have all I need or want in terms of material things. My money concerns are not about what I can buy. My concern is about money to cover our basic needs and the standard of living we are used to.

I worry every day. Rocky continues to spend as if we don't have a worry. My worry is that we have no definite plan as to how we're going to survive financially if we live another 10/15/20 years.

I've decided today, Sunday, May 29, 2011, to be a day of healing. I need to release myself of negative thoughts, attitudes, and financial woes. Financial woes are put on the back burner until tomorrow.

I wonder why am I here? The mental pain can be so intense and can move you to dark and lonely places. You realize only you can save yourself. But do you have the will to do so? My son and my grandsons, I think of them; I get the strength. They provide a will for me to live.

There is also physical pain. My right leg threatens me. It tries to take away my independence by being painful at different levels. Sometimes intense; sometimes mild; always there; controlling my movement.

On this day, Sunday, May 29, 2011, I begin a path of healing, both mentally and physically. I need to be healthy for at least a few more years. I want to see my grandsons grow up and be healthy and strong in mind and body. I need to be here to provide love, support and encouragement.

Striving for 15 more years of a sound mind and a healthy body. In 15 years, Johnnie will be 25, Clinton will be 21, Michael will be 19, and David will be 15. They will be well on their way to becoming strong, happy, and productive young men. Then grandma can rest peacefully as the wind blows her ashes across the earth.

June 21, 2012

8:30 AM this morning, Rocky announced he was leaving to go to Savannah. I was still in bed. He asked if I wanted to go. I said," No". Then he simply went out the front door and drove away.

Wednesday is my day to play cards at the Senior Citizen Center. My morning session playing was fun. We had lunch and chatted before the afternoon session.

It was during the afternoon session when I suddenly began to feel strange. I felt as if my body was experiencing a gradual meltdown. My heart began to pound. I was overwhelmed by fear. I thought I was going to die on the spot. I told the ladies I was feeling weird. They saw a visible change in my demeanor.

Out of concern, EMS was called. My blood pressure was 199. I was shaking like a leaf on a windy day. I took an anxiety pill; EMS said things to help me calm down. They stayed until I recovered from what surely was a full-blown panic attack.

I called Rocky. He was still in Savannah, he called back to check on me. I was fine. I was able to drive home.

When I arrived home Rocky was there. He did not ask any question or express any concern about my ordeal with the EMS guys. He simply watched TV and ignored me for the night, same as he does every night.

I went to the sunroom to watch TV. When he was ready for bed, he turned off all the lights in the house. He and our dog, Suzy, strolled off to bed as usual.

I stayed up much longer and finally got into our king size bed. Rocky sleeps on his side I sleep on my side. There's no physical touching between the two of us.

It's so painful living like this. Some days I just want to die. But thoughts of my beautiful grandsons keep the life light burning within me.

December 10, 2013

Today is December 10, 2013, as I sit here writing, I'm wondering if I will be here next year on December 10, 2014. I am so miserable. My face has turned completely black. I look so awful. I see my image in the mirror; it gives me chills. I look like a monster. I don't like myself. I am so embarrassed. I hate to go out in public.

I wonder if I will survive this ordeal. I want to stay around to see my grandchildren grow up, but I realize that might not be my fate. Life is just so difficult presently.

Is this the feeling people get just before their life comes to an end?

I'm going to see my doctor on Friday. I hope he can provide some help for me. I feel that he will tell me there is nothing he can do, nothing can be done to my face. I am not sure I will be able to live with a face that looks like mine. I need a reason to hope for the future.

June 21, 2017

I have been married 45 years. Have they been happy years? Well, I suppose there may have been happy times, but the truth is my husband has resented and abused me for 45 years. Not physically abused, but controlled, manipulated, and deceived me. The constant mental and emotional beatdown is taking its toll on me.

It has taken me 45 years to finally see the truth and to accept it for what it is. I've always known there was something different about our relationship. I just blamed myself. I did not deserve a loving, kind, and passionate relationship. I was not smart enough, not attractive enough, not good enough for this man to love me. I was just lucky enough that he decided to marry me.

Well, now I'm old and weary. I live in a perpetual state of anxiety and heartache. Sometimes I just want to die. I think about it a lot. Some days it seems that living this way is not worth living it at all. But I have a son and four grandsons. I try to carry on for them. I have begun to break away from the control that my husband has over me. I'm doing more things independently.

My journey; where do I go? Johnnie, Clinton, Michael, and David; I love you all. You are the reasons I continue the struggle to inhale and to exhale.

June 22, 2017

I know I cannot continue to live under these conditions much longer. I need to leave this toxic relationship. I just recently realized I have been emotionally abused for years. One day recently, Rocky called me a nasty bitch. It was on a day when I was feeling so depressed I could barely get out bed.

Rocky shouted at me saying, "You are possessed"! He said, You are not human". He told me I should go and jump into a river. How am I supposed to process these words? They crush my soul. There's an emptiness inside of me. I am broken.

Rocky went to his VA meeting today. When he returned home, he was so angry. I have never seen him that angry before. I tried to talk to him, but he said to get away from him and not to touch him. Then he angrily shouted at me, "I do not like you!" He packed a bag and said he was going away for several days to find some peace. I am wounded. I am lost. I have no clue as to what I have done wrong.

June 23, 2017

As I awake this morning, I'm panic stricken. Rocky left yesterday and stayed away overnight. I have no idea where he is, but the house feels better when he's not here.

The look on Rocky's face yesterday as he shouted at me, "I don't like you!" is etched in my soul. I have no clue as to what I've done that makes him despise me so much.

I know it's not healthy for me to live here, but I have no place to go. My will to live is not good currently. I don't have any plans to kill myself because the impact of suicide would be too much for my grandsons. They're struggling with the possibility of divorce between their parents these days.

Writing helps to calm my nerves a bit for the time being. I need to get ready to go to work at the Bargain Box in a couple of hours. I put a smile on my face and pretend that all is well.

I cannot live with Rocky anymore. He has caused me nothing but pain and heartache from the very beginning until now. I thought his abusive behavior was an expression of love. I was desperate for someone to love me.

Now I realize that he never loved me and does not love me and will never love me. He only loves himself. I've got to find a place to live. I don't want to be part of this kind of relationship. I want to be a part of a kind, loving, peaceful, respectful, and healthy relationship before I die.

Someone in the universe please help me. I so desperately need your help. I need to leave, but I have no place to go. Rocky has had control of all the finances from the day of the marriage. I did not prepare well for retirement. I am dependent upon him financially. I am trapped.

He says I am sick; I am the crazy one; and I need to get help. I do agree because I've been put down and crushed for years. No one survives years of abuse as a sane person.

Naturally, he bears no responsibility whatsoever. There's nothing wrong with him. It's just me and my craziness. He expresses no empathy, shows no affection, no touch, no interaction. I believe he hates me and wants me out of his life.

I need to help my son and his boys get through a divorce and to adjust to a new life. Once that is done, I will concentrate on a new life for myself. I hope I will be able to survive healthy and strong enough for that day to come.

I did research and discovered articles on verbal, emotional, and psychological abuse. As I read, the picture in my mind was defined abuse. Awareness spoke to me, "You are an abused wife." I reflect and view repeated patterns that existed for years. The awareness effected bruises to my soul.

I lived with fear and anxiety all my life. My maternal grandmother was very regimented and controlling. She often enlisted the silent treatment with me. She whipped me when I did not adhere to her rules. One morning I stayed in bed later than usual. My grandmother came into my bedroom with a long switch and whipped me for staying in bed after 8:00 AM.

My maternal grandmother was an abuser. She showed no love for me.

I was weak and fragile when I married Rocky. I was looking for love, happiness, and peace. That was not to be my reality. I married a narcissistic abuser. I left the home of my abusive maternal grandmother and moved on effortlessly into the realm of another abuser.

My journal writings reveal a vivid picture of the pain, the heartache, and the abuse I endured for so many years.

I did not know there was a name for the abuse. When I researched **narcissism**, the causation for the abuse was clearly defined.

I am a victim of Narcissistic Abuse!

On Hilton Head Island, Rocky's public persona was that of a charming, wonderful man and husband. He was totally different at home.

Rocky was stone cold toward me; rarely engaging in a conversation; often using silent treatment. There was no affection, no intimacy and no love shown to me. He told me we discussed topics I knew had never been mentioned. He made decisions I did not know anything about. He spent excessive amounts of money on himself. He bought hats, shoes and shirts that he did not need. He bought the latest computers, Apple watches and Apple phones. He bought an expensive exercise bike. He bought an expensive massage chair. He created thousands of dollars in debt using multiple credit cards. **(Huge RED FLAGS)**

Narcissists are excessive spenders.

Rocky installed cameras with audio sound in the kitchen/dining areas and in the family room at Chinaberry Circle. I did not question his motives. I assumed they were safety measures. I now believe his motive was to spy on me. **(Red flag)**

Narcissists watch their victims.

The 12 years living at Chinaberry Circle caused much suffering. There was so much ongoing emotional, psychological, and mental abuse. I was blindly wandering in a fog searching for a vision of light.

There were many times Rocky said such awful things to me. He called me a bitch numerous times. He said I was possessed. He told me to go jump into a river. He implied I was ugly. He said I was insane. He said I was a terrible person. He said I was a negative person. He said I was crazy. He said he despised me. He said he hated me. **(Red flag)**

I heard these statements spewing from Rocky's mouth I could not understand what was occurring; could not understand the reasons for his expressions of hatred. I did not know what I was doing wrong. I was lost and confused.

Narcissists project and deflect.

I was seeing a psychiatrist, a primary doctor and specialists for various mental and physical illnesses. I told my psychiatrist about what I was experiencing with Rocky. She merely said it appeared to be a communication problem between the two of us. She was so wrong. She apparently did not know about NPD (narcissistic personality disorder).

I often had suicidal thoughts. I did whatever I could do to survive. I joined NAMI (National Alliance for Mental Illness) to help cope. I often parked my car and walked miles on the island. Sometimes I parked my car, got in the back seat, and cried for very long periods of time. I was struggling for survival.

Rocky and I merely lived in the same space on Chinaberry Circle. I wanted him to hear me; to see me; to touch me; to acknowledge my existence. Day after day, he ignored me and made no attempt to interact with me. **(Red flag)**

I was living a nightmare; could not grasp what was happening to me. I craved for him to recognize and to treat me like a human person. He appeared oblivious.

Narcissists devalue victims.

I was so desperate for his affection. There were times when I went to him as he sat on a recliner watching TV. I knelt between his legs, put my head on his chest, and hugged him. I needed some relief. He appeared amused by my expression of love for him. **(Red flag)**

Narcissists withhold affection

I reflect on those times and feel disgust for that pathetic version of me. I was like a puppy lapping at its master's feet.

My physical and mental health began to erode. The stress began to affect my health. My skin began to break out in dark spots and my hair fell out. I could not sleep at night. The only way I could rest was to take prescribed medication and to drink alcohol every night just to fall asleep. I felt that I was slowly dying. **(Red flag)**

I desperately needed a change. I decided to make plans to return to Georgia where Charlie and our grandsons lived. I persuaded Rocky to sell the condo we owned. After the sale, we were able to buy a home in Georgia. We did not move to GA at once; HH Island remained our permanent residence for the time.

Camary Court, Conyers, GA became a nice retreat for me. I went and stayed there for weeks working, decorating, and painting. I enjoyed making changes in the house. I was always so productive when Rocky was not present. I felt free to inhale and to exhale while working at Camary Court, Conyers, GA. **(Red flag)**

Meanwhile, still living at Chinaberry Circle with Rocky was taking a massive toll on me mentally and physically. I became isolated and fearful of ever leaving home. I ordered groceries and had them delivered to the house because I could not leave. Sometimes I was just too afraid to drive my car. The outside world was slowly becoming a frightening place. I had pain in my legs that was so bad that walking was a painful endeavor. I had to force myself to take a shower; it became a weighted undertaking. I was miserable all the time; there was no joy at Chinaberry Circle. **(Red flag)**

I knew I was in serious trouble. I decided it was time to move back to Georgia. Rocky and I agreed to rent Chinaberry Circle and to move to Camary Court, Conyers, GA.

December 2022, Rocky went to Georgia for Christmas holidays. He took the Christmas cards holding money gifts I had prepared for our grandchildren. I chose to remain on Hilton Head Island. I wanted to prepare for the rental of Chinaberry Circle. I painted, decorated and cleaned. I worked diligently every day.

Rocky routinely called me every day. I expected him to call me Christmas Day while he was visiting with the grandchildren. He spent Christmas Day with Charlie and the family. I was alone; no one called to include me as they celebrated Christmas as a family. I felt hurt deeply.

When Rocky returned home to Camary Court, he called. I asked Rocky if he knew how much it hurt me that he did not include me during the Christmas celebration with the family. His abrupt answer was an emphatic, "No". **(Red flag)**

I experienced a gut wrenching feeling of despair. I knew something was off. I was speechless. The conversation ended at that very point. We both hung up.

I waited sleeplessly through the night, hoping Rocky would call me back. I waited the next day and the day after (December 27th, our 51st wedding anniversary). I waited; January 2023 rolled in. I waited three more weeks; Rocky never called. **(Red flag)**.

I did not know the vocabulary at that time; in time I learned; I was "discarded" big time. Which translates to, "I was of no value to him"; "I was not worthy of his time".

That is how a narcissist treats you. They cast you to the side like trash.

(Red flag)

Narcissists discard victims.

In the 51 years we had been married, there had never been more than a day or two of no contact between us. I could not understand why Rocky did not call. During my decades of being with Rocky, I never chased after him. My pride would not allow that to happen. I was suffering, but I refused to call him during that three-week span.

Those three weeks were horrible for me. I had nightmares and panic attacks. I was like an addict needing a fix. My addiction to Rocky was so strong. **(Red flag)**

I knew something was terribly wrong and dysfunctional in our relationship. I began searching and researching to find reasons why a husband hates his wife.

Narcissists punish victims.

Then I began reading about the covert narcissist. Bingo! There were answers I had been looking for. I literally dropped to my knees in anguish and despair. As I read, there was no doubt; Rocky fit the profile.

It was a massive revelation to learn the man I loved; the man I married and lived with for 51 years; was a complete fake. He deceived me for over 52 years.

The Rocky I knew and I loved all those years, suddenly vanished from my reality in December 2022. He would never return. The grief of my loss is a heavy burden I carry every day.

I had so much more to learn about **narcissism** and about the **covert narcissist**. It was months of research and study before I understood the magnitude of my situation.

Once you know the truth about a **covert narcissist**, you can never not know. It was the beginning of the end. The disillusionment of a marriage that was a fake from the very beginning. The pain and grief of the truth is beyond comprehension. I will never recover.

When Rocky returned home after the three-week discard, he was mean-spirited, ice cold and boldly arrogant. I had the following note posted on the bathroom mirror and on the refrigerator:

> *December 2022, when you left, it was us, a team of you and me. Then I simply expressed my feelings of hurt because no one cares to call me on Christmas Day as our family gathers to celebrate.*
>
> *A mere expression of my emotional human feelings gets me abandoned like a piece of trash. Shunned and cast away as if I don't exist. I am devastated. I am broken. My heart hurts. My soul hurts. I hurt.*
>
> *I clearly see a painful picture of a wife, not loved, not valued, not appreciated. What a great beginning for 2023.*
>
> *Know this!*
>
> *I am human! My life matters!*

I am positive Rocky read the note, but he never discussed anything about it with me. **(Red flag)**

He sent a screen shot of it to Charlie. **(Red flag)**

I was weak, broken and tearful. I cried constantly. I cried so much and so frequently that one day Rocky called for medical advice. He led them to believe I was suicidal. **(Red flag)**

Police officers came to the house for a wellness check. If there are no visible wounds, no one will believe you if you tell them you're being abused. They are easily influenced by the charming abuser. He/she is believed; the victim is assumed to be the crazy.

I called Rocky out as being a narcissist. It was a major mistake. He removed the nice guy mask and revealed his true self. I shouted at him, "How could I not know who you really are all these years"? His response, "Because you are stupid". **(Red flag)**

"Because you are stupid", that statement crushed my inner being. I felt as if every part of me just dissolved. There are no words to express the level of pain I felt at that moment. During all these decades being with this man; he merely viewed me as a **"stupid being"**. Those words will resonate in my mind forever. **(Red Flag)**

Narcissists believe they are superior to others.

MY DAY OF MADNESS

February 28, 2023, I was alone at Camary Court. Rocky was at Chinaberry Circle. I was weak, broken, distraught, and disoriented. I had been crying buckets of tears for many days.

In a previous phone call with Charlie, I told him I believed his father was a covert narcissist. Charlie came to Camary Court to discuss the situation brewing between his father and me. I was hoping for support from Charlie. I needed a shoulder to cry on.

Charlie started by reading the definition of "covert narcissist". He expanded to words of defense for his father. **(Red flag)**

I was in an emotional state of extreme grief. Charlie did not express any compassion nor any empathy toward me. **(Red flag)**

He began to criticize me and to question my stability. His words were disrespectful and hurtful. I ended the conversation and directed Charlie to my front door.

The following exchange was recorded on Ring.

Charlie: "You are a covert narcissist!" ***(Red flag)***

Me: "Get out of my house; do not come back; do not contact me!"

Charlie: "You will contact me before I contact you."

Me: "Bullshit!"

Charlie: "I love you." ***(Red flag)***

Me: "I do not love you!" "Get off my property!" "Do not come back!"
"I will call the police!"

Charlie: "You need help!" (Red flag)

"I love you" and **"You need help"** are classic statements commonly spoken by a narcissist. Rocky and Charlie have said them repeatedly to me overtime.

I was a mad woman that day. I was not in control of myself. I was lost in a wilderness of despair.

Less than an hour after Charlie's departure, a young police officer showed up at my front door. He said my son called in for them to do a wellness check on me. **(Red flag)** I assured the officer I was fine. He departed convinced I was okay.

I sincerely feel the real reason Charlie called the police was because I threatened to call the police on him. He had no concern for my well-being. Charlie was sending me a message. **(Red flag)**.

I look at my son and think, this man is the baby I carried nine months! He is now someone I do not recognize. It breaks my heart that Charlie disrespects me and berates me. I am his 76 years old mother. How can this be my reality?

I tolerated Charlie speaking to me in disrespectful ways for many years. I had no choice; he is 52 years old. His words too often brought tears to my eyes. I could not understand why my son could be so cruel to me. He addresses me by my given name, Veronica. Deleting the title of mommy, mama or mom from me broke my heart. It equates to having motherhood taken from me. I am so perplexed. What did I do to deserve this kind of treatment from my only child.

Charlie is quite aware of the pain caused when he calls me Veronica. He appears to relish it. Charlie's behavior contributes to my feeling of worthlessness.

Narcissists thrive on causing pain.

Rocky has not been diagnosed to be a covert narcissist, but I know that he is. I did my homework. I have the experience, the pain, and the unseen wounds that define narcissistic abuse.

Rocky will never seek help because in his delusional mind he is simply perfect. All the problems in our relationship are my fault. I am one who needs help. That is the mindset of a person with NPD. They always blame others; they are never responsible for any wrong doings.

A narcissist strives to keep his/her victims under control under any means possible.

Rocky knows I am afraid of snakes. A mere picture of one effectuates fear and anxiety for me. Rocky killed a venomous snake in our backyard. I was away from home at the time. He texted me a picture of the dead snake hanging from a tree. There were no words, just the picture of the snake. **(Red flag)**

I did not see the text before I arrived back home. When I got home, I went outside to pick some tomatoes. Rocky shouted to me, "Do you see the snake?" I shouted in fear, "What snake?" and ran back into the house. The dead snake was hanging from the tree I had just walked pass. **(Red flag)**

Be aware, a narcissist will prey on your weaknesses.

I did not know for decades the extent of the toxicity in my marriage. That is not uncommon when dealing with a covert narcissist. They deceive people skillfully. They lie masterfully. A relationship with a covert narcissist can last for decades before you realize who really lurks behind the mask of deception. **(Red Flag)**

I thought Rocky was the best husband any woman could ever have. I was so proud to be his wife. He meant the world to me. I was so messed up. I thought he deserved someone smarter and prettier than me. I lived in constant fear that a female would come along and take Rocky from me. **(Red flag)**

I was in love and enchanted with the false persona Ricky maintained so well. The person lurking behind the mask remained well hidden from me for decades. **(Red flag)**

I doubt there will ever be a full recovery from the narcissistic abuse I endured; the wounds are too deep. They are profoundly devastating and are beyond comprehension. The only people who can fully understand what narcissistic abuse is like are those of us who experienced it. I am not alone. There are many (male and female) suffering and struggling to survive.

I empathize with anyone who has NPD (narcissistic personality disorder). Their life is in constant chaos trying to identify self. They hurt so many people because they're self-centered. Their wants, desires, and needs are all that matter. They must abuse and they must deceive other people in order to feel good about themselves. Sad life to live for a narcissist and even sadder life for those of us who love and live with them.

CAMARY COURT

We move to Camary Court in March 2023. By this time, I was a total wreck and in constant emotional, mental and physical pain. The excruciating pain plagued me throughout the year of 2023. I screamed out to the universe, "How can this be my reality"? My mind, my body, and my soul experienced pain every minute of my waking hours. There was no escape, no relief.

I had suicidal thoughts so often. I had visions of the guns I knew were in a drawer on Rocky's side of the bed. I did not trust myself to look at them.

My mind and my body were slowly breaking down. I lost 30 lbs. within a few months. My hair continued to fall out. The person looking back at me from a mirror was a haggard old woman whom I did not recognize.

There were constant arguments between Rocky and me. I was naively seeking and demanding explanations and clarifications from him. This merely fueled his rage. After one heated argument, a cruel stranger shouted at me, "Eat shit and die!". Those words resonated to my soul and confirmed the hatred this man feels for me. I was completely broken and devastated.

Yet, I blindly held on to the hope that some parts of the Rocky I loved and adored still existed.

In time it proved to be fruitless hope. This was a stranger who lived in the home with me; the person who lurked behind the mask revealed himself every day. The Rocky I knew was gone forever. **I will grieve the loss for all eternity.**

IS THERE A GENETIC LINK TO NPD?

GRANDDFATHER (ROCKY'S DAD)

Rocky's father abused his mother during their marriage. Rocky and his siblings recalled troubling times during their childhood. (Red flag) *There were rumors of Rocky's father making inappropriate advances toward teenage girls.* (Red flag) *Rocky's youngest sister believes their father touched her inappropriately when she was a young child. It greatly affected her life.* (Red flag)

I always felt uncomfortable in the presence of Rocky's father. I felt an instinctive aura of evil around him. Now I have that same instinctive aura of evil feeling around Rocky. (Red Flag)

Rocky's father boldly moved his girlfriend to an apartment just walking distance from where he resided with Rocky's mother. (Red flag) *After 36 years of marriage, Rocky's mother got a divorce. Rocky's father immediately married his younger girlfriend* (Red flag).

When we visited the couple, the wife was always scurrying around trying to please Rocky's father. She was always a nervous wreck. (Red flag) *It was obviously displayed by her tone and by her actions. They remained married for many years until the day she died suddenly of a massive heart attack.*

Narcissistic abuse is destructive and life threatening.

Grandson (Rocky's and my son)

Our son, Charlie, was married about 12 years when he began complaining about his wife. He made statements about her that caused me to believe she was the problem. (Red flag) *I blindly sided with Charlie against his wife.*

Charlie began a long-distance affair with his former college girlfriend. She lived in Pennsylvania. She was divorced and was raising two children. She entered the affair knowing Charlie was married and living with his wife and children. That fact did not seem to matter to her. He said he wanted to marry her. (Red flag)

Charlie continued to paint the picture of his wife being the problem in the marriage. I foolishly believed whatever Charlie said just like I had done so many times with his father. The situation became so stressful, Charlie's wife filed for a divorce.

It was a contemptuous divorce. Charlie was rageful and angry. He wanted to make his wife's life miserable. (Red flag)

I continued to blindly support Charlie until the divorce was final.

Charlie and his girlfriend made immediate plans for their wedding. They got married very quickly after the divorce was finalized. (Red Flag) *The new Wife and her two children moved to Georgia.*

THE YEAR 2023

My emotions were confounding in 2023. My thinking was not always rational. I joined several groups on Facebook that addressed narcissism.

I received numerous posts every day about narcissism. I began reposting a flurry of information on narcissism. Sometimes, I would share three or four in one day.

The act of posting the information provided a sense of relief; it was a form of therapy for me. I wanted people to become aware of narcissism and NPD. I confess; I wanted others to know I was living with it. I wanted others to know I was suffering.

There was never any direct reference to Rocky. I confess to wanting others to make their own inference regarding Rocky.

Charlie made the inference. On October 13, 2023, Charlie posted a flurry of his own on Facebook. My heart broke into a million pieces.

CHARLIE'S RAGE I

If a bear broke into your yard and ravaged your yard, ate your chickens 40 YEARS AGO, you should have dealt with that bear at that time. Since then, you allowed the bear to stay in your yard and he softened up and y'all worked it out and lived life. So now, 40–50 years later you start opening old wounds, poking the Bear constantly. When the bear growls, you run to social media and cry what a horrible narcissist the bear is. Consistently poking the bear and attempting to isolate the bear via social media posts is narcissistic in itself. Remember, I'm the chicken in the yard (not some flying monkey). I've observed both sides. Told you about it and was run off along with other family members. When you point the finger at everybody else, sometimes it's not everybody else, it's you. You.

II

Well let me retort. I posted it because you can't have civil conversations. I can only stand and watch for so long. In my case, the last time we spoke, I came to you calmly and told you that you needed help. I held up a mirror to you. I asked you if you were sure he was the narcissist or are you. Instead of listening, you started talking over me and shouting at me. Then you threw me out of your house. All these strangers who don't know you, have no idea the ordeal it's been over the years. I am witness to both sides. I'm not denying that my father has not been the perfect spouse over the years. He had his hang ups. Most of which happened 40 and 50 years ago. He hasn't been that person for decades. Those who know him can see it. You've baited us and when we respond, you claim victim. It's in one of your own posts. That's narcissistic behavior according to your own post. At least on FB, you can't shout and drown people out. I only want what's best for both of you. I think it's unfair to poke the bear and play victim when the bear responds. For those new folks in her circle, please continue to pray for her and my father. Also encourage her to go back to the help she stopped taking a year and a half ago. Since then, this situation has continued to escalate. I'm sorry that this all comes out on FB. It impacts my entire family. She stopped speaking to us earlier this year and we still love her and wish her the very best. Lastly, we're not flying monkeys if we disagree with her. We're all capable of independent thought. I base my conclusion on the evidence presented. One more thing, MY FATHER IS NOT A NARCISSISTIC ABUSER.

III

Veronica Harvin stop playing victim instead of doing what's necessary to make you well doesn't help your situation. Your behavior has impacted my wife and kids. You know what you stopped doing to make you well. This thing has escalated since you stopped. I've tried to tell you and for my trouble I was shouted down and thrown out of your home. I love you and want what's best for you, but you have to seek professional help and get yourself back together. I'm here to help. You can't hold civil conversations. You seem to respond to FB messages. 2 way communication works much better than 1 way.

IV

These therapeutic solutions of airing dirty laundry for public speculation, damage other people. That's not productive in any way. I appreciate that you have people who support you. I'm a supporter too, however, I have witnessed both sides of the story. I think a professional solution was diagnosed for you years ago. You stopped following professional advice over a year ago. Please get back on track with the professional solution prescribed to you. Your behavior in the real world as well as the FB reality has damaged and impacted your loved ones. We love you.

I was working as a substitute teacher on October 13, 2023. It was the teacher's prep period; there were no students in class. I looked on Facebook and saw Charlie's first post to me. I was shocked by the content of what I read. I became nervous, anxious and tearful. My heart was deeply wounded; it shattered into painful pieces.

Warrior that I am, I regained my outer composure as the students entered class. My inner self was crushed and pained. It was a long, enduring, and painful day at school. Later that day, I responded to Charlie's first post in this way:

> *Family and friends who care, support, and believe me; trust that I speak Truth! I am suffering and struggling to survive.*
>
> *My son directed this post to me. I rest my case on narcissistic abuse! Please pray for him, for Rocky, and for me.*
>
> *Veronica Harvin*
>
> *October 13, 2023*

I did not respond to Charlie's other three posts that followed.

Charlie's posts sparked a series of phone calls and text messages from family and friends to Rocky and to me. I heard from childhood friends I had not seen, nor had I spoken with for over fifty years.

I was so grateful and thankful to all the kind people who reached out to me. However, they did not understand the complexity of the situation. They thought my son was expressing concern for his mother. Their view of the situation was misconceived. My son was expressing narcissistic rage.

The one resounding theme conveyed by everyone concerned for our family was that we should not address personal family issues via Facebook.

Most people have no awareness and no knowledge of narcissism and narcissistic abuse.

I hope people will read my story and gain some understanding of this bizarre disorder: **narcissistic personality disorder.**

I saw Charlie at an event on December 16, 2023. Charlie did not look well to me. I was moved by my maternal instincts to make peace with my son, Charlie.

I wrote Charlie a note of apology. I bought a special Christmas card, placed the note and a one hundred dollar bill inside the card.

Rocky delivered it to Charlie on Christmas Day.

There was no acknowledgment nor response from Charlie to me. I suppose in Charlie's way of thinking, his mother no longer exists. That is the way he treats me; he ignores my existence. There is no way to describe my pain.

Rocky told me Charlie and Charlie's wife were upset with me because I did not include the wife with my gift to Charlie.

My Note to Charlie

AN APOLOGY TO MY SON

November 10, 1971, the day you were born, happiness was abound because I experienced true love. I was blessed with the delivery of a beautiful, healthy baby boy. It was the beginning for you and me, a family of two. I was content.

However, I was young and vulnerable. I had already ignored so many red flags that were waved at me before you were born. I was easily lured back into a relationship that blinded me to reality.

I married your father on December 27, 1971. That date sealed our fate, plunging us into a world of fantasy created by a master manipulator. Mama did not protect you because she had no clue as to whom she actually married. I am so sorry, son. Your mother failed you.

Over the decades we were manipulated, controlled and deceived. Here we are, 52 years later, struggling to survive the damage that has been done to you, to me, and has extended to your children. I am okay with the fact that you don't believe me nor agree with me. I totally understand your reasoning.

I am aware that you and your father want to get a court order to say I am unstable simply because you two can no longer manipulate and control me. I am not the one who is unstable.

The pain I have endured the past few months is almost unbearable. The love I have for your children is the driving force that keeps me going every day.

I have formed a no contact policy with you because it is best for me. When I saw you last night. My maternal instinct kicked in. You did not look well to me. Your Mama wants you to be well and to be happy. However, there is nothing I can do to save you. That breaks my heart. You must save yourself and keep yourself healthy. I will always be your mother from a distance.

Love,
mama

Intuition

My intuition warned me that 2023 would be the worst year of my life. It was the first year without the man I had loved for the past 53 years of my life; without the man who protected me; without the man who soothe my wounds. He was gone forever. I grieve for him every day. It was a rude awaking to a new and unfamiliar world. It was like being lost in the wilderness.

I often doubted I would survive to see 2024. 2023 was a year of intense pain and anguish. I was a broken Humpty Dumpty; pieces that could never be put back together again. Every minute of my waking hour was consumed by depleting anguish. I lived in an endless nightmare.

I literally fell to my knees time and time again screaming out for mercy. I wanted someone to come to save me; to deliver me from the utter anguish that plagued my being. I wanted the Rocky I knew and I loved to come to save me. Knowing that was impossible, because my Rocky never existed. My Rocky was a mere illusion, a false being, a fictitious character who existed only in the fantasy world he created.

It is so difficult for the mind to comprehend that humans with NPD really do exist. Yet, they do. We are just not educated about their disorder.

There were often thoughts of suicide. Love for my grandchildren kept those thoughts from becoming actions.

This was my state of being during the year of 2023. It was the worst year of my 76 years on Earth. I survived; **"What an amazing feat!"**

Journal Writing 2023

July 12, 2023

Rocky tried to harm me today. He was in a state of rage after we had an argument in the car. I exited the car and walked toward entrance to the opened garage door. Rocky suddenly and purposely closed the door. I walked through the door as it was coming down and got my head banged. I entered my home, my place of safety, feeling very unsafe.

August 5, 2023

Today is August 5th, 2023. I am so weary and tired. I am trying to stay away from Rocky as much as possible. He is so mean and abusive toward me. He told me he hates me. He demonstrates that hate by the way he speaks to me and by the way he pronounces my name. No one can imagine the devastating pain I feel knowing I live with someone who devalues me and thinks that I am worthless. This life is almost unbearable.

October 8, 2023

This morning as I prepared to go to work as a substitute teacher, Rocky said, "Did you eat anything?"

Me: "Do you really care?"

Rocky, "No!" "Why are you so nasty?" "You know I care." (My soul feels the pain of Rock's toxic words).

Me: "How am I being nasty, Rocky?" I walk away.

I beg the universe for strength to survive this journey of perpetual narcissistic abuse.

That afternoon when I returned home from work, Rocky observed photos of him and me that I had turned backwards. I reversed the photos because I did not want to look at them. Rocky shout out, "Bitch"! I knew he was referring to me. I confronted him. He questioned why the pictures were reversed. I gave no explanation. He left to attend a football game. When he returned, he did not acknowledge me nor talk to me.

October 9, 2023

Rocky got up very early this morning. I got up and prepared to go to work as a substitute teacher. When I went into the kitchen, there were three pots of boiling water on the stove. Rocky did not acknowledge my presence. I was fearful. I quickly made my exit to go to work.

October 22, 2023

I recently learned that Rocky and Charlie were plotting to have me declared unstable because I posted so many articles on Facebook about narcissism and narcissistic abuse.

I am so lost. I don't know where to go, what to do. My life is total madness. My son and my husband express so much hate toward me. I have always loved them and supported them in every way possible for all these decades we've been together. My life does not matter to them.

Rocky is so charming and likeable; friends and family won't believe my story. I must be okay with that. I speak the truth. I have travelled this journey of abuse with Rocky. He has manipulated, abused, used, controlled and deceived me for so long.

The past 15 years have been the worst. I have been discarded and devalued time and time again. Yet, I tried to hold on, tried to please him, tried to love him in every way. Always hoping he would show me something in return; some reciprocity. Years of no affection, no intimacy, and no touching, break a person's will and reduce them to an empty feeling of worthlessness.

I had panic attacks, anxiety, depression, and sleepless nights. I would tell him I was hurting; he just ignored me. There were times he called me awful names and said things about me that are not true.

Here I am today, trying to process thoughts racing through my mind. How can I continue to live with a person who acknowledges no value to my life? A man who has poisoned my only child's mind against me. Rocky has told Charlie so many negative things and untruths about me.

It is so sad because our son, Charlie, is a victim just like me. He does not realize what his father has done to both of us.

I feel as if I failed my son because I did not protect him from the abuse that began the day I married his father.

Rocky took my baby from me and used him as his little "flying monkey". My son hates me because Rocky programmed him to believe whatever he wanted him to believe.

Now I have no contact with Charlie. It is for my own mental health that I distanced myself from him. Charlie is as abusive toward me as Rocky is.

October 23, 2023

I had a restless night. Can't clear my mind of the thought that Rocky and Charlie were plotting to have me put away in a mental place.

Rocky admitted that they were planning something. He said he told Charlie to put a halt to it. Rocky said he could not live with himself if they followed through with the plan. He would not tell me the details of their plan.

I don't know what they might do to me. I don't feel safe. I need help; I am so alone. I pray to the universe to see me through this ordeal.

I keep thinking and thinking; there must be a way for me to safely escape and to live a happy life before I die.

I stay only for financial reasons. I don't get enough money monthly to be able to pay rent and to pay other living costs. I drive the car that is not paid off; Rocky would stop payment and have the car repossessed if I were to leave.

I feel so trapped. I would never have believed this is the way my life would end.

CALL TO THE POLICE

December 21, 2023, I confess; I baited Rocky. I brought up subjects that caused him much distress. I suggested we get a divorce. Rocky became extremely agitated. He walked out to the deck.

Rocky never hid his phone nor password from me. It was common for me to use his phone. This night when I picked up his phone, it was different. Rocky rushed inside and snatched his phone. I said, "Oh, you have something to hide!" I followed Rocky to the bathroom; I demanded his phone. He gave it to me and he demanded my phone.

Rocky took my phone and slammed it against the headboard of the bed. His expression was horrifyingly vile; a look I had never seen. I fell back to the floor in shock and disbelief. Rocky retrieved his phone and proceeded to take a picture of me. I jumped up, snatched his phone and moved toward the family room. Rocky tackled me to the floor. As we both landed, Rocky's head hit against the hearth. There were specks of blood.

I was terrified. I tried to use my Apple Watch to call 911. The vile looking stranger ripped the watch from my arm. I ran through the garage to a neighbor's house and called 911.

Narcissists are dangerous.

Rocky met the two police officers as they arrived. He spoke to them before I returned from my neighbor's house.

Rocky made a call to Charlie.

I told an officer my version. I expected some concern for my welfare. The officer asked if I had been drinking. I said I had one glass of wine and that Rocky had one glass of wine, also.

The other officer was talking with Rocky when Charlie arrived. We all went inside the house. I was told I could write a report. I was so nervous and disoriented I could barely remember how to spell.

Charlie told the officers I was off my meds and was showing signs of dementia. This is the tale Rocky and Charlie told anyone who would listen. It was obvious the officers believed Charlie and Rocky. Four men, Rocky, Charlie and two officers glared at me as if I were insane.

The officers suggested one of us leaves the house for the night. Rocky went home with Charlie. My son, Charlie, walked away smiling as if he had won the Super Bowl. I was left alone, a defeated team of one.

I will never call the police again; no matter what happens. I called them because I was in distress. They told me we both could be arrested. I understand why people fear the police.

The Year 2024

All during the year of 2023, I watched videos, read documents, devoured all information I could find on narcissism, covert narcissists and narcissistic abuse. I educated myself to gain some level of understanding of NPD. I needed to know about this strange man I married and with whom I lived for decades.

I spent hours, days, weeks, and months constantly seeking knowledge. One day I reached a level of truth and recognition. Then finally, acceptance; with acceptance came some relief.

In March 2023, moving from Chinaberry Circle to the Camary Court, I carefully packed my car. I put all my meds into a large clear plastic bag. I unloaded my stuff into the garage at Camary Court. Later, I searched and searched for the bag of my meds. I could not find them anywhere in the garage.

There were multiple bottles of duloxetine, bupropion, buspirone, and trazadone. All prescribed by my psychiatrist. I had been ingesting them into my body for years trying to cope with panic attacks, anxiety, and depression. I eventually weaned myself from all of them. I manage very well without them now that I know what and whom I am dealing with in my life.

Around the time my meds went missing, Rocky and I had a heated argument; he went into a rage. It suddenly hit me! Rocky threw my meds away during his state of rage. That was a logical explanation. I confronted Rocky. He stated if he threw them away, he did not remember. **(Red flag)**

"I do not remember" is a common statement spoken by a narcissist.

Well, fast forward to January 2024. I asked Rocky to set aside some boxes from Chinaberry Circle that were not opened. When I checked in the garage, I saw a large open container Rocky had set aside. As I rummaged through the container, my heart stopped. Inside the container was the long-lost bag of my meds. I was overcome with emotions. I had accused Rocky of disposing of my meds; yet, right before my eyes was the bag of meds.

I went to Rocky; I tearfully apologized. Rocky was as cool as a cucumber. He merely shrugged it off and voiced no response. He boldly turned away from me as I stood there distraught and remorseful. He did not utter one word. **(Red flag)**

I doubted myself; thinking perhaps, I was wrong about other issues with Rocky, as well. **(Red flag)**

Narcissists love to play mind games with their victims.

Those emotions I was feeling lasted about a hot minute. Then my senses brought me back to reality. This is the man who lurked behind the mask for decades deceiving me. I almost got lured back into his manipulative game again. My bag of meds had been hidden away all those months. **(Red flag)**

Fortunately, I had long weaned off all the meds. I was managing better without ingesting my body with the toxicity of pills. I threw the bag into the trash.

My composure regained, I calmly said to Rocky, "I was once naive and perhaps stupid. I educated myself; I am no longer naive nor am I stupid". No response from Rocky. **(Red flag)**

PRESENT TIMES

There has been no communication between Charlie and me since my day of madness when I demanded Charlie leave my property. I recently saw a text Charlie sent to Rocky in reference to me. Charlie wrote, "I am through with her!" "Good luck to you!" There are no words to express my hurt, my pain, nor my anguish. I am so puzzled by my son's actions toward me.

Narcissists hold grudges.

It cannot be normal for a son to treat his elderly mother with such disdain. I can only conclude that over time Rocky has continuously fed Charlie enormous portions of poisonous lies about me. The rift Rocky has meticulously crafted between my only child and me is unforgivable. That is the vile behavior of a covert narcissist.

Narcissists triangulate.

I currently live at Camary Court with Rocky. We share this space because we are connected financially. There is no love, no peace, no happiness at this address.

I moved from the master bedroom to the other side of the house where there is a Jack/Jill bedroom setting. I feel more at peace now that we no longer sleep in the same bed.

Rocky does not wear the mask with me. I live with the person who lurked behind the mask all this time. He is not nice, not loving, not kind, and not charming. He ignores me most of the time. Unfortunately, I am the only person who knows the true Rocky, the man who lurks behind the mask of deception.

When others are present, Rocky easily slips on the mask. People see his charm. They are convinced he is nice and he is kind. I watch with feelings of annoyance and disgust at the blatant deception.

However, I accept the fact that people are free to judge Rocky on the basis of who he presents himself to be to them. That is a reality of life.

No one will believe the truth about Rocky's true character. I totally understand the feelings of others. They can only make judgements about Rocky in terms of their interactions and experiences with him. I have the highest regards and respect for all Rocky's friends and family. They only know the masked version of Rocky he so eloquently displays to the public. I am sure it will be difficult for them to believe my story.

I understand, accept, and respect whatever response comes with sharing my story. I know the Rocky Hudson who lurks behind the mask. You do not want to meet him.

Rocky and I rarely talk to each other. In Rocky"s delusional world, I am not worthy of engaging in a conversation with him. He has devalued and discarded me. I am dead to him.

I must admit, there were times, out of pure frustration, I baited him. I brought up something from the past. He became enraged. **Narcissistic rage** is a frightening scene to watch and to experience. I have learned my lessons; I no longer say anything that elicits **narcissistic injury** (threat to his entitled self-image).

Rocky says I am a terrible person. I am convinced that in Rocky's delusional mind, he views me as this terrible person whom he hates with a vengeance. His actions and his words convey how he despises me.

People cannot imagine the pain and heartache those of us who experience narcissist abuse endure. We know the narcissist in our lives has no empathy, no compassion, and no love for us. We live with that knowledge every day.

I honestly don't feel safe. I know Rocky is vengeful and he holds grudges. I fear what he does behind my back. I must tread cautiously in his presence. I am careful what I say because he is easily offended and becomes defensive and deflective. His actions, words, and tone convey hatred.

Life with a narcissist is an extremely agonizing and difficult way to live your life.

I remain here because I am old; I am weary. Rocky is old and weary. There is no affordable place for either of us to flee. We are both so miserable.

I go to work several days during the week as a substitute teacher just to stay away from Rocky.

I remind Rocky that he needs me and I need him. Rocky takes care of the cars and the yard. He does all the laundry. I prepare meals and cook. I remind Rocky that we must strive for a peaceful coexistence here on Camary Court. Rocky agrees. However, I know you can never trust the words of a narcissist. I remain forever hypervigilant.

My story has an ending that is yet to be told. I seek peace, love, and happiness for my conclusion.

NPD (narcissistic personality disorder) is a perplexing disorder. I do not think Rocky is aware that what he does is harmful to others, nor that his actions cut deep wounds that never heal. He appears oblivious and exhibits no care. He is content with himself as long as his needs, wants, and desires are met.

Rocky hurts me so much. Yet, I feel empathy and compassion for him. He is the only man I have ever loved. I will always feel love for Rocky despite all the pain that I have endured all these years.

Rocky will always be a part of me; I am bonded to him forever. I will never be free. I will never be free of Rocky Hudson.

This is what can potentially happen to you if you love someone who has NPD; if you love a narcissist. Please take notes and learn from my story.

AFTERTHOUGHTS

Life is a path traveled from birth to death. The journey is uniquely different for everyone. My path began with a father who discarded his wife and two children and never looked back. My mother, unable to cope, left my brother and me in the care of an abusive grandmother.

My journey has been a desperate search for love. I thought I found that love with Rocky Hudson. I was trauma bonded to this man for so long. I often told him he was my mother; my father; my sister; my brother; my everything. Rocky meant the world to me.

It is difficult to explain the relationship with the narcissist. It is strangely different from other relationships. You always sense that something is off; never quite right. The narcissist believes he/she is this uniquely grand person. He/she feels superior to others.

Narcissists are in fact quite unique. They appear to have a unique ability to cast a spell on victims. They lure you in with their charming persona. When they have you hooked, they use and abuse you until they become bored with you. They want a new challenge, so they discard and abandon you. They ignore you as if you never existed. They move on quickly to the next victim. You're left stunned, disoriented, and broken.

Narcissists do not love others. They cannot form true connections with other people. They are too absorbed in themselves. Narcissists love only what others can do for them. The relationship with the narcissist is always transactional. There is always a selfish motive for their actions.

Rocky stayed with me all those years. Because I was good supply for him. I was a hard-working wife with a steady paycheck. I was loyal, faithful, and obedient. Our relationship showed the public he was a good family man.

Narcissists get bored very easily. Rocky obviously became bored with me very early in the marriage. That is why he constantly sought after other women to satisfy his wants, needs, and desires.

However, a narcissist's wants and desires are never satisfied. There is an empty void inside that can never be filled.

A narcissist will always chase to find the person to fill the emptiness; the person to bring happiness to their miserable lives. The chase will be in vain because the next person will never be enough for the Narcissist. The chase will continue endlessly.

Narcissists are never satisfied.

My journey did not take me along a life path of love as I had hoped it to be with Rocky. It was a long path of manipulation, control, deception, and pain.

An irony of a relationship with a narcissist is that the narcissist causes pain and anguish. Yet, the narcissist is the only person who can soothe the pain and anguish you feel. It equates to a junkie needing a fix.

Narcissists are addictive.

I guess I am lucky Rocky did not abandon me like my father did. My father just left town one day with another woman never to return. He left behind a wife, a son and a daughter. He easily discarded us as if we never existed.

I truly believe if Rocky had left me for another woman, I would not have survived the devastation of his abandonment. I suspect I would have committed suicide. In my world, Rocky meant life for me. In my mind, my heart, my soul; there was no life without Rocky. I felt that way for decades.

There is a strong trauma bond that develops when you love a narcissist. You are like a slave trapped in bondage; paralyzed with fear and insecurity. Your master, the narcissist, is your lifeline.

Narcissists traumatize victims.

Writing my story has been a painful undertaking. There was so much about my life with Rocky and the unusualness of the relationship revealed to me. So much that was unnoticed and unacknowledged until now.

I do not understand how I lived with Rocky all those years and never realized he never loved or cared about me. I do not understand how I allowed myself to be used, controlled, manipulated, deceived, and disrespected for so long. I grieve every day for the loss of so much.

I continue to shed many tears because the pain embedded so deeply within will not release itself from me. The only people who will understand and relate to the pain and anguish are the ones who have experienced narcissistic abuse.

Writing my story might be considered an act of selfishness or even an act of vengeance. My intent is neither selfish nor vengeful. I want to bring awareness to the woes of narcissistic relationships. Narcissistic relationships will destroy you.

I doubt that recovery is possible for some of us. I am old; I endured for 52 years; there is no recovery for me.

Writing my story was a goal I set for myself. It is an achievement I reached for myself. I feel very proud of myself. It makes me feel my life matters.

Veronica Harvin

Postscript

Friday, March 8, 2024

Rocky had an MRI on Tuesday. He met me at the garage door when I returned home from work. He said he had bad news. Someone from the hospital called and informed him that the MRI revealed a growth on one of his kidneys.

Rocky printed out the MRI results. I read the report. Rocky has renal cysts on one of his kidneys. These results caused some concern to doctors. Rocky might have a procedure done to reduce the size.

I don't know what this means in terms of Rocky's health. However, I remain committed to Rocky. If he is sick, I will always provide him with the best care in every way possible.

I will never abandon him in his hour of need.

Veronica Harvin

9 798892 850766